D1109606

Textbook

Level 1

Siegfried Engelmann
Elaine C. Bruner

A Division of The **McGraw-Hill** *Companies*

Columbus, Ohio

Illustration Credits

Olivia Cole, Mark Corcoran, Len Epstein, Kersti Frigell, Meryl Henderson, Susan Jerde, Loretta Lustig, Jan Pyk, and Gary Undercuffler.

www.sra4kids.com

SRA/McGraw-Hill

A Division of The **McGraw·Hill** *Companies*

Send all inquiries to:
SRA/McGraw-Hill
8787 Orion Place
Columbus, OH 43240-4027

Printed in the United States of America.

ISBN 0-07-569015-2

1 2 3 4 5 6 7 8 9 RRC 06 05 04 03 02 01

Table of Contents

arf the shark

arf was a barking shark. arf was a little shark, but shē had a big bark that māde the other fish swim awāy.

a shark swam up to arf and said, "you are a shark. let's plāy."

arf was happy. "arf, arf," shē said. and the other shark swam far, far awāy. arf was not happy now.

another shark swam up to arf. "you are a shark," hē said. "let's plāy."

arf was happy. "arf, arf," shē said. and the other shark

swam far, far awāy. arf was not happy now.

then a big, big fish that līked to ēat sharks swam up to the other sharks.

"help, help," they yelled.

but the big fish was swimming after them very fast.

stop

arf can help

arf was a barking shark. the other sharks did not like her big bark. when arf went "arf, arf," the other sharks swam away.

but now arf had to help the other sharks. a big fish that liked to eat sharks was going after the other sharks. arf swam up to the big fish and said, "arf, arf." the big fish swam far, far away.

the other sharks liked arf now.

"we like arf now," they said.

and now arf plays with the other sharks. and if a big fish

that līkes to ēat sharks swims up to them, arf says "arf, arf." and the big fish swims far, far awāy.

the end

rēad the Items

1. when the tēacher stands up, clap.
2. when the tēacher claps, hōld up your hand.

---

lIked	barking	when
swim	that	there
fōr	hēre	other
get	shē	funny
got	they	hōrse
end	where	cāme
and	how	give
at	whȳ	trȳing
āte	dōn't	rIding
ēat	didn't	hard

109

rēad the Ītem

when the tēacher says "stand up," sāy "gō."

the cow boy and the cow

a cow boy was sad. hē did not have a hōrse. the other cow boys said, "hō, hō, that funny cow boy has nō hōrse."

a cow cāme up to the cow boy. the cow said, "if you are a cow boy, you nēēd a cow. I am a cow."

the cow boy said, "do not bē funny. cow boys do not rīde on cows."

the cow said, "but I can run as fast as a hōrse. and I can jump better than a hōrse."

the cow boy said, "I will give you a trȳ. but I will fēēl very funny rīding on a cow." sō the cow boy got on the cow.

then the other cow boys cāme up the rōad. "hō, hō," they said. "look at that funny cow boy. hē is trȳing to rīde a cow."

stop

rēad the ītem

when the tēacher says "now," pick up your book.

the cow boys have a jumping mēēt

the cow boy got on a cow. the other cow boys said, "hō, hō. that is funny."

the cow boy got mad. hē said, "this cow can gō as fast as a hōrse. and shē can jump better than a hōrse."

110

the other cow boys said, "nō cow can jump better than mȳ hōrse." sō the cow boys rōde to a crēēk.

the cow boy on the cow said, "let's sēē if a hōrse can jump this crēēk."

"I will trȳ," a cow boy said. his hōrse went up to the crēēk. but then his hōrse stopped. and the cow boy fell in the crēēk.

the cow boy on the cow said, "hō, hō. that hōrse didn't ēven trȳ to jump the crēēk."

the next cow boy said, "mȳ hōrse will trȳ. and mȳ hōrse will flȳ ōver that strēam.

hē will not ēven touch the strēam."

mōre to come

111

rēad the ītem

when the tēacher says "stand up," hōld up your hand.

the cow boys trȳ

some cow boys māde fun of a cow boy that rōde a cow. they said, "nō cow can jump better than a hōrse." sō they rōde to a crēēk to sēē if a cow could jump better than a hōrse.

a cow boy fell in the crēēk. now the next cow boy was gōing to māke his hōrse jump ōver the crēēk. his hōrse went very fast. the hōrse cāme to the bank of the crēēk. then the hōrse jumped. did hē gō to the other sīde? nō, hē went splash in the crēēk. the cow boy was mad.

the next cow boy said, "I will trȳ to jump ōver that crēēk. and I have the best hōrse in the land."

but that cow boy's hōrse went splash and the cow boy fell in the crēēk. the cow boys said, "wē did not jump that crēēk, but that fat cow can not jump as far as a hōrse."

"let's sēē," said the cow boy with the cow. the cow started to run faster and faster and faster. the cow ran up to the bank of the crēēk. and then the cow jumped.

stop

rēad the Item

when the tēacher says "clap," touch your fēēt.

the happy jumping cow

the cow boy on the cow was trying to jump ōver the crēēk. the cow ran to the bank and jumped with a big jump.

the cow jumped ōver the crēēk. the cow did not touch the strēam. the other cow boys looked at the cow. they said, "we are wet and cōld." but the cow boy on the cow was not wet. and hē was not cōld.

112

hē gāve the cow a kiss. and hē said, “now I fēēl līke a rēal cow boy. thōse other cow boys can have a hōrse. I will stāy with this jumping cow.” and hē did.

hē rōde the cow. hē jumped ōver rocks with the cow. hē had that cow fōr yēars and yēars. and nō other cow boy ever māde fun of his cow after the cow jumped ōver the crēēk.

the end

rēad the Items

1. when the tēacher stands up, sāy "gō."
2. when the tēacher says "do it," hōld up your hands.
3. when the tēacher says "stand up," hōld up your hand.

113

of
fōr
and
how
other
strēam
this
hēre
there
whȳ

better
faster
you
didn't
crȳing
flȳing
after
things
gōing
touch

circle
farmer
start
where
when
them
then
what
that
thōse

rēad the Items

1. when the tēacher says "do it," touch your fēēt.
2. when the tēacher stands up, hōld up your hands.

jill and her sister

this is the stōry of a girl nāmed jill and her sister. jill trIed to do things, but her sister did not trȳ.

jill said, "I can not rIde a bIke, but I will trȳ."

what did jill sāy?

her sister said, "I can not rIde, but I do not lIke to trȳ."

soon jill rōde a bīke, but her sister did not. her sister started to crȳ. jill said, "if you trȳ, you will not have to crȳ."

then jill said, "I can not jump rōpe, but I will trȳ."

what did jill sāy?

her sister said, "I can not jump rōpe, but I do not līke to trȳ."

soon jill jumped rōpe, but her sister did not. her sister said, "I can not jump rōpe, sō I will crȳ."

jill said, "if you trȳ, you will not have to crȳ."

mōre to come

rēad the Items

1. When the tēacher claps, touch your head.
2. When the tēacher says "clap," touch your fēēt.

jill trIed and trIed

did jill trȳ to do things?

did her sister trȳ to do things?

What did jill do when shē trIed?

jill said, "I can not rēad a book, but I will trȳ."

What did jill sāy?

her sister said, "I can not rēad a book, but I will not trȳ."

what did her sister sāy?

sō jill trīed to rēad and her sister did not trȳ.

now jill is good at rēading. but her sister can not rēad books. her sister can not rīde a bīke. her sister can not jump rōpe. and her sister can not rēad books. but her sister can do some thing better than jill. her sister can rēally crȳ.

this is the end.

116

rēad the Items

1. When the tēacher stands up, pick up your book.
2. When the tēacher stands up, touch your head.

jon bākes a fish cāke

a boy nāmed jon was gōing to bāke the best cāke hē ever māde. hē said, “I will trȳ to bāke a fish cāke.”

hē asked his brother, “will you help mē bāke a fish cāke?”

What did hē ask?

his brother said, “ick. a fish cāke? I hāte fish cāke.” hē ran into the yard to plāy.

jon askₑd his sister, "will you help mē bākₑ a fish cākₑ?"

what did jon ask?

his sister said, "ick. a fish cākₑ? I rēally do not līkₑ fish cākₑ." then his sister ran into the yard to plāy.

jon ēven askₑd his mother, "will you help mē bākₑ a fish cākₑ?"

what did jon ask?

but his mother said, "ick. fish cākₑ? ick."

sō jon mādₑ the fish cākₑ him self.

mōrₑ to come

116

rēad the Ītems

1. when the tēacher says "clap," touch your nōse.
2. when the tēacher says "gō," sāy "fīve."

jon hātes fish cāke

what kīnd of cāke did jon bāke?

did his sister help him?

did his mother help him?

jon māde the fish cāke bȳ him self.

when hē sat down to ēat the cāke, his brother cāme in. his

brother asked, "can I trȳ some of that fish cāke?"

what did hē ask?

jon said, "you didn't help mē bāke the cāke, sō you dōn't have to help mē ēat it."

jon's mother and jon's sister cāme in. they asked, "can wē trȳ some of that fish cāke?"

what did they ask?

jon said, "you did not help mē bāke the cāke. sō you dōn't have to help mē ēat the cāke."

sō jon āte the fish cāke bȳ him self. then hē got very sick. now hē hātes fish cāke. if you ask him to help you bāke fish cāke, hē will sāy, "ick. I hāte fish cāke."

What will hē sāy?

the end

118

rēad the ītems

1. when the tēacher stands up, sāy "you are standing up."
2. when the tēacher claps, pick up your book.

spot

this is a stōry of a dog nāmed spot. spot did not hēar well. the other dāy shē went to a stōre to get some bōnes. the man in the stōre said, "it is a fīne dāy."

"what did you sāy?" spot asked.

tell spot what the man said.

the man got some bōnes fōr spot. hē said, "pāy mē a dīme fōr thēse bōnes."

spot asked, "what did you sāy?"

tell spot what the man said.

spot did not hēar the man and the man was getting mad at spot. the man said, "give mē a dīme fōr thēse bōnes."

spot asked, "what did you sāy?"

tell spot what the man said.

spot said, "it is tīme fōr mē to lēave. sō I will pāy you a dīme fōr the bōnes and I will gō hōme."

118

sō spot gāve the man a dīme.
then shē took the bōnes hōme
and had a fīne mēal of bōnes.

the end

rēad the Ītem

when the tēacher hōlds up a hand, touch the flōōr.

spot and the cop

this is another stōry of spot the dog.

did spot hēar well?

one dāy spot went fōr a walk to the other sīde of town. when shē got there, shē said, "I can not fīnd mȳ wāy back hōme."

what did shē sāy?

shē walked and walked. but shē did not fīnd the strēēt

119

that led to her hōme. shē started to crȳ.

then a big cop cāme up to her. spot said, "Ī trīed and trīed, but Ī can not fīnd mȳ wāy back hōme."

the cop said, "where do you live?"

spot said, "what did you sāy?" tell spot what the cop said.

spot still did not hēar what the cop said. sō the cop got a pad and māde a nōte fōr spot. the nōte said, "where do you live?"

spot read the nōte and said, "Ī live on broom strēēt."

the cop said, "I will tāke you to broom strēēt." and hē did. spot kissed the cop and said, "some dāy I will pāy you back. you are a good cop."

the end

120

rēad the ītems

1. when the tēacher stands up, pick up your book.
2. when the tēacher says "touch your fēēt," touch your fēēt.

the boy asked whȳ

a boy nāmed don līked to ask whȳ. his mother tōld him to stāy in the yard. hē asked, "whȳ?" sō shē tōld him whȳ. shē said, "wē will ēat soon." what did shē sāy?

don dug a big hōle in the yard. his brother said, "you must not dig hōles in the yard."

don asked, "whȳ?" sō his brother tōld him. his brother said, "hōles māke the yard look bad." what did his brother sāy?

don got a can of whīte pāint. "I will pāint mȳ bīke whīte," hē said. sō hē got the pāint brush and started to pāint his bīke.

his sister asked, "what are you doing?"

don answered, "pāinting mȳ bīke whīte."

what did the boy sāy?

mōre to come

rēad the Ītem

when the tēacher stands up, sāy "stand up."

don pāinted and pāinted

what did don lĪke to ask? what did hē do in the yard? what did hē start to pāint? who asked him what hē was doing with his bĪke?

his sister said, "that looks lĪke fun." sō shē got a pāint brush and started to pāint don's bĪke.

don and his sister pāinted the bĪke. then don said, "whȳ

dōn't wē pāint the sīde walk?"

what did hē sāy?

sō they pāinted the sīde walk.

what did they do?

then they pāinted the steps to don's hōme.

then they pāinted a rock.

and then they pāinted ēach other.

then don's mom went into the yard. shē was mad. shē said, "you pāinted the bīke, the steps, the rock, and ēach other."

what did shē sāy?

what do you think shē did to don and his sister?

the end

rēad the Ītems

1. when the tēacher says "fēēt," touch your fēēt.
2. when the tēacher says "stand up," hōld up your hands.

spot helps the cop

spot was walking nēar a stōre. robbers cāme from the stōre with bags of monēy. a big cop ran to stop the robbers. hē yelled, "drop that monēy." but the robbers did not drop the monēy. the robbers had a big hōrn and they started to blōw it. "toot, toot," the hōrn went.

"I can not stand the 'toot, toot' of the hōrn," the cop said. "it mākes mȳ ēars sōre."

the cop held his hands ōver his ēars. then the robbers ran bȳ him. the hōrn was still gōing "toot, toot."

the hōrn did not māke spot's ēars sōre. spot did not ēven hēar the hōrn. sō spot ran up to the robbers. spot bit them on the legs. they dropped the big hōrn. they dropped the monēy. then the cop stopped them.

hē said to spot, "you helped stop the robbers." what did hē sāy?

the big cop was very happy.

the end

rēad the ītem

when the tēacher picks up a book, sāy "hands."

flȳing is fun

a little bird had six sisters. his sisters said, "come and flȳ with us." but the little bird did not flȳ. sō hē started to crȳ.

his sisters said, "wē did not sāy to crȳ with us. wē said to flȳ with us. stop crȳing and start flȳing."

but the little bird did not stop crȳing.

his sisters said, "whȳ are

you crȳing?" what did they sāy?

the little bird said, "I am crȳing bēcause I cannot flȳ."

whȳ was hē crȳing?

his sisters said, "wē will tēach you to flȳ if you stop crȳing."

sō the little bird stopped crȳing. then his sisters grabbed him and took him up, up, up into the skȳ.

then they said, "you are a bird, sō you can flȳ."

they let gō of him. hē yelled, "I can flȳ."

now when the sisters sāy "let's flȳ," the little bird jumps

up and down. hē says, “yes, flȳing is mōre fun than crȳing.”

then the little bird and his sisters flȳ and flȳ.

What do they do?

the end

rēad the ītems

1. when the tēacher says "go," sāy "fīve."
2. when the tēacher stands up, sāy "now."

the farmer and his buttons

a farmer līked buttons. he had red buttons and gōld buttons. he had lots of big buttons and lots of little buttons. he had buttons on his hat and buttons on his socks. he ēven had buttons on some of his buttons. but he had his best buttons on his pants. he had ten big buttons on his pants.

one dāy a man cāme to the farm. the man said, "I have come to buȳ buttons." he looked at the buttons on the farmer's pants. "I will buȳ that big red button," he said.

so the farmer took off the big red button and sōld it. now he had nīne big buttons on his pants.

then the man said, "now I will buȳ that big gōld button."

so the farmer took off the gōld button and sōld it. now the farmer did not have nīne buttons on his pants. do you think the man will buy more buttons from the farmer?

more to come

rēad the ītem

when the tēacher says "go," touch your head.

the farmer sōld his buttons

what did the farmer līke?

where did he have his best buttons?

what did the man want to bu̅y from the farmer?

the man kept bu̅ying buttons and the farmer kept selling them. the man said, "now you have fīve buttons. I want to bu̅y that pink button." so the farmer took off his pink button and sōld it to the man.

125

then the man wanted to buȳ the farmer's yellōw button. so the farmer sōld the yellōw button to the man.

the man said, "you still have thrēē buttons. I will buȳ them."

so the farmer took off the thrēē buttons. but when his pants had no mōre buttons, his pants fell down. what did they do?

the farmer said, "mȳ pants fell down bēcause I sōld the buttons that held up mȳ pants." what did he sāy?

so now the farmer has monēy, but he has no buttons to

kēēp his pants up. how will he kēēp his pants up?

this is the end.

126

rēad the Item

when the tēacher says "clap," touch your fēēt.

spot tākes a trip

one dāy spot said, "I want to go on a trip in mȳ car." so she did.

she got in her car and went down the rōad. soon she stopped. she asked a man, "where can I get gas?"

the man said, "on best strēēt."

spot said, "where did you sāy?"

tell spot what the man said.

so spot went to best strēēt and got gas. then she went down the rōad some mōre. soon she stopped. she asked a lādy, "where is the town of dim?"

the lādy said, "dim is fīve mīles down the rōad."

spot asked, "where did you sāy?"

tell spot what the lādy said.

and spot went to the town of dim. then spot stopped and asked a man, "where is a stōre that sells bōnes?"

the man said, "go down to māin strēēt."

"where did you sāy?" spot asked.

tell spot what the man said.

so spot went to the stōre and got a bag of bōnes. she had a good trip.

the end

rēad the Items

1. when the tēacher says "what," touch your nōse.
2. when the tēacher stands up, sāy "sit down."
3. when the tēacher says "do it," hōld up your hands.

127

park	hēre	calling
are	whȳ	hall
shark	līkes	of
barn	wanted	for
farm	stopped	thōse
what	very	thēse
want	ēven	that
were	all	them
where	fall	they
there	call	when

rēad the ītem

when the tēacher says "now," clap.

the dog līkes to talk, talk, talk

a tall man had a dog that līked to talk and līked to rēad.

one dāy the dog was rēading a book. the tall man was in the hall. he called the dog. he yelled, "dog, come hēre and plāy ball with me."

the dog yelled back at the man, "ī hēar you call, call, call, but ī dōn't līke to plāy ball, ball, ball."

the man was getting mad. he yelled, "dog, stop rēading that book and start plāying ball."

she yelled, "I will not go into the hall, hall, hall, and I will not plāy ball, ball, ball."

the man was very mad now. he cāme into the room and got his cōat. he said, "well, I am gōing for a walk. do you want to come with me?"

the dog said, "I will not do that, that, that, when I can sit hēre and get fat, fat, fat."

so the tall man left and the dog went back to her book. she said, "I hāte to walk, walk,

walk, but I like to talk, talk, talk."

the end

129

rēad the ītem

when the tēacher says "do it," hōld up your hand.

the small bug went to live in a ball

there was a small bug that did not have a hōme. he went to live in a tall trēē. but a big ēagle said, "this is mȳ tall trēē. go look for another hōme."

then the bug lived in a hōle. but a mōle said, "that's mȳ hōle. go look for another hōme."

then the small bug lived on a farm in a box of salt. but a cow said, "that's my salt. go away or I'll eat you up when I lick my salt."

then the small bug lived in a stall on the farm. but a horse said, "what are you doing in my stall? go find another home."

at last the bug went to a home near the farm. he spotted a ball on the floor. the ball had a small hole in it. the bug said, "at last I see a home for me." he went into the ball and sat down. he said, "I hope that I can stay in this ball. I like it here."

more to come

129

rēad the Item

when the tēacher says "go," sāy "stand up."

the bug in the ball mēēts a girl

a small bug had a hōme in a ball. he said, "I hōpe I can stāy in this ball. I līke it hēre."

he went to slēēp in the ball. he was having a good drēam. he was drēaming of a fīne party. then he sat up. the ball was rōlling. "what is gōing on?" he called.

he looked from the little hōle in the ball and saw a tall

girl. she was rolling the ball on the floor.

"what are you doing?" he asked. "this is my home. stop rolling it on the floor."

the girl picked up the ball and looked at the small bug. then she dropped the ball. "oh," she cried, "there is a bug in my ball. I hate bugs."

the ball hit the floor. it went up. then it went down. then it went up. the bug was getting sick.

"stop that," he called. "I don't like a home that goes up and down."

the tall girl bent down and looked at the bug. she said, "this is mȳ ball. so go awāy."

the small bug looked up at the girl and started to crȳ.

mōre to come

131

rēad the Item

when the tēacher stands up, sāy "you are standing up."

the bug wants to stāy in the ball

a small bug wanted to live insIde a ball. but a tall girl tōld him that he must lēave the ball and fInd another hōme. the small bug started to crȳ. he said, "where will I go? I cannot live in a tall trēē. I cannot live in a box of salt. I cannot live in a hōrse stall. and now I cannot stāy in this ball."

"stop crȳing," the girl said. "I can't stand to sēē small bugs crȳ."

the bug said, "if you let me stāy in this ball, I will plāy with you."

"no," the girl said. "I dōn't plāy with bugs. I hāte bugs."

the bug said, "I can sing for you. I will ēven let you come to the party that I am gōing to have in mȳ ball."

she said, "dōn't be silly. I can't fit in that ball. look at how tall I am."

the bug called, "let me stāy."

the girl sat down on the

floor and looked at the small bug. "I must think," she said. What was she going to think over?

more to come

read the Item

when the teacher says "go," touch your arm.

the tall girl bets her brother

a tall girl wanted the bug to leave the ball and find another home. the bug cried and told her all the things he would do if she let him stay in the ball. he said that he would sing for her. he said that he would let her come to his party in the ball.

the girl was sitting on the floor thinking of the bug.

then her brother cāme into the room. he said, "What are you doing?"

she said, "go away. I am thinking."

he said, "do you think that the ball will start rōlling if you look at it very hard?" her brother did not sēē the bug inside the ball.

the girl said, "if I want this ball to start rōlling, it will start rōlling. and I dōn't ēven have to touch it."

her brother said, "I'll bet you can't māke that ball rōll if you dōn't touch it."

"how much will you bet?" the girl asked. she looked at the bug and smīled.

her brother said, "I will bet you one football and ten toy cars."

the girl said, "I will tāke that bet."

mōre to come

132

rēad the Item

when the tēacher says "stop," touch the flōōr.

the tall girl wins the bet

the tall girl māde a bet with her brother. she bet him that she could māke the ball start rōlling. she said, "I dōn't ēven have to touch it."

her brother did not sēē the bug in the ball. so he bet one football and ten toy cars.

the girl looked at the ball and said, "start rōlling, ball." the bug started running inside the ball. he ran and ran. he ran so fast that the ball started to rōll.

the girl's brother looked at the ball. he said, "wow. that ball is rōlling and you are not ēven touching it."

the girl said, "I tōld you I could māke the ball rōll."

so the girl got one football and ten toy cars.

then she said to the small bug, "you helped me win the bet, so I will let you stāy in mȳ ball. this ball is your hōme now."

the bug was so happy that he ran from the ball and kissed

the girl on her hand. "thank you, thank you," he said.

and nēar the end of the wēēk, he had a fīne party insīde his ball. every bug on the strēēt cāme to the party, and they all said that it was the very best party they ever had.

the end

133

rēad the Item

when the tēacher says "go," hōld up your hands.

the elephant gets glasses

a small elephant was not happy bēcause he alwāys fell down.

one dāy he went for a walk. he could not sēē the tall trēē. so he hit his head on the tall trēē and fell down.

he said, "whȳ do I alwāys fall down? I wish I would not fall. I hāte to fall."

134

he walked some mōre. he could not sēē a big red ball. so he fell ōver the big red ball.

the small elephant said, "whȳ do I alwāys fall down? I hāte to fall."

he walked some mōre. but he could not sēē all the boys and girls ēating hot dogs. he could not sēē the pīle of hot dogs. so he fell into the hot dogs.

the boys and girls got mad. "how could you fall into thōse hot dogs?" they said. "do you nēēd glasses?"

the elephant said, "I have never sēēn glasses."

so a tall girl took her glasses and gāve them to the elephant. the elephant trīed on the glasses.

"mȳ, mȳ," the elephant said. "now I can sēē all kīnds of things. I can sēē tall trēēs, balls, and hot dogs."

now the small elephant is happy bēcause he has glasses. and he never falls down.

this is the end.

the dog loves to rēad, rēad, rēad

a dog that could talk lived with a tall man. the dog took a book from the table. the dog said, "this book is what I need, need, need. I love to read, read, read."

the tall man came in and said, "I look, look, look, but I cannot see my book, book, book."

then the man said, "my book was on the table."

the dog said, "the book was on the table, but I took it from the table."

the tall man yelled at the dog.

he said, "you must not tāke mȳ book from the tāble."

she said, "do you want to plāy ball, ball, ball in the hall, hall, hall?"

"yes, yes," the man said.

the dog kicked the ball far, far, far down the hall. when the man ran after the ball, the dog took the book and hid it.

then she said, "let the man look, look, look. he will never fīnd his book, book, book."

the end

136

walter wanted to plāy football

walter loved to plāy football. but walter could not plāy well. he was small. and he did not run well. when he tried to run with the ball, he fell down. "dōn't fall down," the other boys yelled. but walter kept falling and falling.

when walter ran to get a pass, he dropped the football. "dōn't drop the ball," the other boys yelled. but walter kept dropping balls.

dāy after dāy walter tried to plāy football, but dāy after dāy he fell down and dropped the ball.

then one dāy, the other boys said, "walter, you can't plāy ball with us any mōre. you are too small.

you alwāys fall. and you alwāys drop the football."

walter went hōme and sat in his yard. he was mad. he said to himself, "I am small and I cannot run well." walter wanted to crȳ, but he didn't crȳ. he sat in his yard and felt very sad. when his mom called him for dinner, he said "I dōn't want to ēat. I must sit hēre and think."

mōre to come

136

137

walter gōes to the big gāme

walter was sad bēcause the other boys would not let him plāy football with them. walter was still sad on the dāy of the big football gāme. the boys that lived nēar walter were plāying boys from the other sīde of town.

walter went down to the lot where the boys plāy football. he said, "I can't plāy in the gāme bēcause I alwāys fall. but I will look at the big gāme."

there were lots of boys and girls at the football lot. some of them were chēēring for the boys that lived nēar walter. other boys and girls were chēēring for the tēam that cāme from the other sīde of town.

the gāme started. there was a tall boy on the other tēam. that tall boy got the football and ran all the wāy down the lot. he scōred. the boys and girls from the other sīde of town chēēred.

walter's tēam got the ball. but they could not go far. they went fīve yards.

when the other tēam got the ball, the tall boy kicked the ball. it went to the end of the lot for another scōre. walter said to himself, "that other tēam is gōing to win. I wish I could help mȳ tēam."

mōre to come

7

138

walter gōes in the gāme

walter was looking at the big football gāme. walter's tēam was not doing well. the other tēam had 2 scōres. but walter's tēam did not have any scōres. as the gāme went on, walter's tēam started to plāy well. walter's tēam stopped the tall boy when he got the ball. then walter's tēam scōred. walter chēēred. he yelled, "get that ball and scōre some mōre."

but then the best plāyer on walter's tēam cut his arm. he left the gāme. walter said to himself, "now we cannot win the gāme. the best plāyer is not plāying."

how could walter's tēam win if the best plāyer was not plāying?

then all the boys on walter's tēam started to call. "walter, walter," they called. "come hēre."

walter ran to his tēam. one of the boys said, "walter, we nēēd one mōre plāyer. so we called you. trȳ to plāy well. we nēēd 2 scōres to win this gāme."

mōre to come

138

walter's tēam must kick

walter's tēam called him to plāy in the big gāme.

one of the boys on walter's tēam said, "we cannot run with the ball, bēcause the best runner is not in the gāme. so let's trȳ to scōre bȳ kicking the ball."

"yes, yes," the other boys said.

then the boys looked at ēach other. "one of us must kick the ball."

all the other boys said, "not me. I can't kick the ball that far."

but walter didn't sāy "no." he said, "I will trȳ. I think I could kick the ball that far."

one of the boys said, "I will hōld the ball for him."

139

so walter got ready to kick the ball. some boys and girls called from the sīde of the lot, "dōn't let walter do that. he can't plāy football. he will fall down."

but walter said to himself, "I will not fall. I will kick that ball." and walter felt that he would kick the ball.

mōre to come

walter kicks the ball

walter was ready to kick the ball. the boys and girls on the sīde of the lot were sāying, "dōn't let walter kick."

but walter did kick. another boy held the ball. a tall boy from the other tēam almōst got to the ball, but walter kicked the ball just in tīme. the ball went līke a shot. it went past the end of the lot. it went ōver a tall wall that was next to the lot. it almōst hit a car that was on the strēēt.

the boys on walter's tēam looked at walter. the boys on the other tēam looked at walter. one boy from the other tēam said, "that ball went all the wāy ōver the wall. I did not think

140

that a small boy could kick a ball so far."

the boys and girls on the sīde of the lot chēēred. "that's the wāy to kick, walter," they called.

now walter's tēam nēēded one mōre scōre to win the gāme.

mōre to come

141

walter's tēam wins

the other tēam did not scōre. so walter's tēam got the ball.

one boy on walter's tēam said, "we must go all the wāy down the lot to scōre. but we dōn't have tīme and we can't kick the ball that far."

walter said, "I think I can kick the ball all the wāy." so the boys on walter's tēam got ready.

the ball went into plāy. a boy from walter's tēam held the ball, and walter kicked it. it went all the wāy to the end of the lot. it almōst hit the wall that was next to the lot.

the boys on walter's tēam picked him up and yelled, "walter kicked for a scōre." the boys from the other tēam said, “you are some football plāyer.”

and the boys and girls on the sīde of the lot called, “walter is the star of the gāme.” walter was very happy.

and now walter can plāy football with the other boys any tīme he wants.

the end

rēad the Items

1. when the tēacher says "one," hōld up one hand.
2. when the tēacher says "go," stand up.

---

mad	walter	other
māde	wall	another
hōpe	plāyer	there
hop	picked	what
fin	dropped	that
fīne	cannot	want
all	can't	went
almōst	do	were
also	dōn't	where
alwāys	didn't	whȳ

143

carmen the cow

this is a stōry about a cow nāmed carmen.

when the other cows said "moo," the children alwāys cāme to pet them. but when carmen said "moo," all the children alwāys ran awāy. the children ran awāy bēcause carmen had a loud moo. she trīed to sāy a little moo, but her moo was alwāys a big, loud moo.

the other cows made fun of her. they said, "we do not līke you bēcause your moo is so loud."

carmen trīed and trīed, but her moo was too loud.

one dāy some children cāme to the farm with a tēacher. they cāme to pet the cows. they petted all the

143

other cows, but they did not pet carmen bēcause they did not līke her loud moo.

one of the children started to run up a hill, but she fell in a dēēp, dēēp hōle. she shouted for help. but the tēacher did not hēar her calls. the other cows trīed to help her. they called "moo, moo," but the moos were not very loud, and the tēacher did not hēar them.

mōre to come

143

carmen calls for help

who cāme to the farm to pet cows?

why didn't the children pet carmen?

who fell into a dēēp, dēēp hōle?

how did the other cows trȳ to help the girl?

whȳ didn't the tēacher hēar the cows mooing?

then carmen saw the girl. carmen called "moo" very loud. she called "moo" so loud that the tēacher could hēar her. the tēacher said, "that sounds līke a call for help." the tēacher ran to the little girl.

the tēacher helped the little girl get out of the hōle. the tēacher went ōver to carmen and said, "we are so glad that you have a loud moo. you said 'moo' so loud that you sāved the little girl."

and what do you think the little girl did? the little girl kissed carmen and said, "thank you for mooing so loud."

now carmen has lots of children pet her. carmen is happy that she has a big, loud moo.

this is the end.

jill's mouse

jill had a pet mouse. her mouse was little and pink. jill got a little box for her little mouse. then she went to her mother and said, "look what I have. I have a pet mouse in this box."

her mother jumped up. her mother said, "get that mouse out of this house."

jill said, "but I want to kēēp this mouse."

her mother said, "you can't kēēp that mouse in this house. I dōn't līke that mouse."

jill asked, "would you let me kēēp this mouse in the yard? then the mouse would not be around you."

"yes," her mother said, "but kēēp that mouse out of this house."

so jill took the box and went to the yard. she said, "I will māke a house for this mouse." so she pīled some grass around the box.

now jill is happy and her mother is happy. and the mouse is happy.

whȳ was jill happy?

whȳ was her mother happy?

whȳ was the mouse happy?

the end

146

1

the magic pouch

there was a little girl who lived nēar a tall mountain. the mountain was so tall that the top was alwāys in the clouds. the girl wanted to go to the top of the mountain, but her mother tōld her, "no." she said, "that mountain is stēēp. you would fīnd it very hard to get to the top."

but one dāy the little girl was sitting and looking at the mountain. she said to herself, "I would līke to see what is in thōse clouds at the top of the mountain. I think I will go up and see."

so the girl took her pet hound started up the tall mountain. ent up and up. the sīde of the mountain was very stēēp. up they went. the girl said to her hound, "do not fall. it is very far down to the ground."

soon the little girl and her hound cāme to the clouds nēar the top of the mountain. she said to her hound, "now we will see what is on the other sīde of thōse clouds."

what do you think they will see on the other sīde of the clouds?

more to come

2

the magic pouch

where did the little girl live?

what did the girl want to do?

who tōld her not to go up the mountain?

who did she tāke with her?

where did the girl go with her hound?

the little girl and her hound went into the clouds. she said, "I cannot see too well. thēse clouds māke a fog" but the girl and her hound kept gōing up and up.

all at once they cāme out of the clouds. they could not see the ground any mōre. they could ōnly see clouds under them. they were in the sun. the sun was in the girl's eyes, so she could not see well. she sat down and said to her hound, "we must sit and rest."

all at once the little girl looked up and saw a funny little house. she said, "I didn't see that house bēfōre. let's go see who lives there."

so the girl and her hound walked ōver to the funny little house.

all at once a loud sound cāme from the house.

mōre to come

147

3

the magic pouch

where did the little girl and her hound go?

what did they see when they came out of the clouds?

what did they hear coming from the house?

when the loud sound came from the house, the little girl stopped. she looked all around, but she did not see anyone. the sound came from the house once more. the girl and her hound walked up to the house. she called, "is anyone inside that house?"

all at once the door of the house opened. the girl looked inside the house, but she did not see anyone. slōwly she walked inside. slōwly her hound walked inside. then the dōōr slammed bēhind them. the hound jumped. the girl jumped. she said, "let's get out of hēre." she grabbed the dōōr, but it would not ōpen. the girl said, "I dōn't like this."

all at once the girl looked at a funny pouch hanging on the wall. and a loud sound cāme out of the pouch. it said, "ōpen this pouch and let me out."

mōre to come

148

4

the magic pouch

what did the little girl and her hound see on top of the mountain?

whȳ didn't they lēave the funny house?

what was hanging on the wall?

the girl walked ōver to the pouch. she said, "is there some thing in that pouch?"

"yes. I am a magic elf. I have lived in this pouch for a thousand yēars. plēase, would you ōpen the pouch and let me out?"

the little girl asked, "how many yēars have you lived in that pouch?"

the elf said, "a thousand yēars."

the girl started to ōpen the pouch. then she stopped. she said, "elf, I dōn't think I should let you out. this is not mȳ house. I should not be hēre."

the elf said, "this is mȳ house. so plēase ōpen the pouch and let me out. if you let me out, I will give you the pouch. it is magic."

the girl touched the pouch. she asked herself, "should I ōpen this pouch and let him out?"

mōre to come

5

the magic pouch

what was inside the pouch?

how many years had the elf lived in the pouch?

the little girl said to herself, "should I open this pouch?" she looked at the pouch. then slowly she opened it. out jumped a little elf, no bigger than your foot. the girl's hound went, "owwwww." then the elf jumped all around the room. he jumped on the table and on the floor. then he ran up one wall and down the other wall. he even ran around the hound. "owwwww," the hound yelled.

"I'm out. I'm out," the elf shouted. "I lived in that pouch a thousand yēars and now I'm out."

at last the girl's hound stopped gōing "owwwww." the elf sat on the tāble and said, "I thank you very much. plēase tāke the magic pouch. but be cāreful. when you are good, the pouch will be good to you. but when you are bad, the pouch will be bad to you.

mōre to come

6

the magic pouch

the elf tōld the little girl, "when you are bad, the pouch will be bad to you."

the girl picked up the pouch. she said to the elf, "I have been good to you. let's see if this magic pouch will be good to me."

she rēached inside the pouch and found ten round rocks that shine. "thēse round rocks are gōld," she shouted. "I'm rich."

so the girl thanked the elf for the pouch.

then the girl and her hound started down the tall mountain. they went down and down. they went into the clouds. when they left the clouds, the girl could see the ground. down and down they went.

when they reached the bottom of the mountain, the sun was setting. it was getting late. the girl was tired. but she ran to her house.

her mother met her at the door. she said, "where were you? your father and I have looked all around for you."

the little girl did not tell her mother where she went. she said, "I went to sleep in the grass. I just woke up." she told a lie, and that was bad.

more to come

151

152

7

the magic pouch

did the little girl tell her mother where she was?

what did she tell her mother?

what does the pouch do when you are bad?

the girl's mother looked at the pouch. she said, "where did you get that pouch?"

"I found it on the ground," the little girl said. she tōld another līe. "but mother, there are ten rocks of gōld in this pouch. we are rich."

she rēached in the pouch and took something out. but when she looked, she saw that she was not hōlding gōld rocks. she was hōlding yellōw mud. her mother said, "you are not funny. we are not rich. but you are dirty. go clēan your hands."

the little girl got a rag and trīed to rub the yellōw mud from her hands. but it would not come from her hands. she rubbed and rubbed, but the yellōw mud stāyed on her hands. her mother trīed to get the mud from her hands, but she could not do it.

then the girl started to crȳ.

mōre to come

152

8

the magic pouch

what did the little girl take from the pouch?

could she get the yellōw mud from her hands?

could her mother get the yellōw mud from her hands?

the girl crīed and crīed. then she said, "mother, I tōld you some līes. I did not slēēp in the grass. I went to the top of the tall mountain. and I did not fīnd the pouch on the ground. a funny elf gave it to me." the girl tōld her mother all about the funny house and the elf.

and when she looked at her hands, she saw that they were clēan.

her mother said, "where did the mud go?"

"I dōn't see it any where," the girl said. she looked to see if there was more mud inside the pouch. and what do you think was inside the pouch? there were a thousand rocks of gōld. her mother said, "we are rich. we are very rich."

and the little girl said to herself, "that pouch is good to me bēcause I was good. I will kēēp on doing good things." and she did. and every time she was good, she rēached in the pouch and found something good.

no more to come

154

the bugs and the elephant

five elephants went for a walk. one elephant was very tall. that elephant said, "I must sit and rest. I will look for a spot of ground where I can sit."

so she looked for a good site to sit on the ground. at last she came to a fine site that was in the sun. she said, "this spot is fine." but a flȳ was sitting in that spot. the flȳ said, "go awāy, elephant. this is mȳ spot."

the elephant said, "hō, hō. you cannot stop me if I want to sit in the sun."

so the elephant sat down. that flȳ got out of her wāy. then the elephant said, "this is a fine site. it is fun here."

the fly said, "you took my spot. so I will fix you."

the fly went away and the elephant went to sleep.

when the elephant woke up, she saw that there were many bugs on the ground. those bugs were all around her.

the elephant said, "how did these bugs get here?"

the little fly said, "these bugs are with me. they are here to take you away."

and they did. they picked up the elephant and took her to the lake. then they dropped her in the lake.

now the fly is sitting in the sun and the elephant is sitting in the lake. the fly thinks it is fun to sit in the sun. and the elephant thinks it is more fun to sit in the lake.

this is the end.

the pet gōat

a girl got a pet gōat. she liked to go running with her pet gōat. she plāyed with her gōat in her house. she plāyed with the gōat in her yard.

but the gōat did some things that made the girl's dad mad. the gōat ate things. he ate cans and he ate canes. he ate pans and he ate panes. he ēven ate capes and caps.

one dāy her dad said, "that gōat must go. he eats too many things."

the girl said, "dad, if you let the gōat stāy with us, I will see that he stops ēating all those things."

her dad said, "we will trȳ it."

so the gōat stāyed and the girl made him stop ēating cans and canes and caps and capes.

155

but one dāy a car robber came to the girl's house. he saw a big red car nēar the house and said, "I will stēal that car."

he ran to the car and started to ōpen the dōōr.

the girl and the gōat were plāying in the back yard. they did not see the car robber.

more to come

156

the gōat stops the robber

a girl had a pet gōat. her dad had a red car.

a car robber was gōing to stēal her dad's car. the girl and her gōat were plāying in the back yard.

just then the gōat stopped plāying. he saw the robber. he bent his head down and started to run for the robber. the robber was bending ōver the sēat of the car. the gōat hit him with his sharp hōrns. the car robber went flȳing.

the girl's dad ran out of the house. he grabbed the robber. "you were trȳing to stēal mȳ car," he yelled.

the girl said, "but mȳ gōat stopped him."

"yes," her dad said. "that gōat saved mȳ car."

the car robber said, "something hit me when I was trȳing to stēal that car."

the girl said, "mȳ gōat hit you."

the girl hugged the gōat. her dad said, "that gōat can stāy with us. and he can ēat all the cans and canes and caps and capes he wants."

the girl smiled. her gōat smiled. her dad smiled. but the car robber did not smile. he said, "I am sore."

the end

156

jane wanted to flȳ, flȳ, flȳ

a girl named jane said, "I want to flȳ, flȳ, flȳ in the skȳ, skȳ, skȳ."

her father said, "but if you fall on your head, head, head, you'll end up in bed, bed, bed."

but the girl did not stop talking about flȳing. one dāy she went to her dad and said, "if you help me make a big kite, I can flȳ in the skȳ like the birds."

her dad said, "I will help you make a kite, but I dōn't think you should trȳ to flȳ."

jane said, "that is good, good, good. let's make a kite of wood, wood, wood."

her dad said, "we'll nēēd pāper and string to make this thing."

157

Jane and her dad got pāper and string and wood. they made a kite that was very, very big.

Jane said, "When the wind starts to blōw, blōw, blōw, just see me go, go, go."

her father said, "no, no, no."

more to come

158

jane goes up, up, up

a girl named jane wanted to flȳ, but her dad didn't want her to flȳ. he helped her make a big kite. but he tōld her that she could not flȳ with that kite.

then one dāy, the wind started to blōw. jane got her big kite. she said, "I dōn't knōw whȳ, whȳ, whȳ dad wōn't let me flȳ, flȳ, flȳ."

as she was hōlding the kite, a big wind started to blōw the kite awāy. jane said, "I must hōld on to that kite or it will go far awāy."

so she held on to the kite. but when the wind started to blōw very hard, it lifted the kite into the skȳ. she looked down and yelled, "I want mȳ dad, dad, dad, bēcause this is bad, bad, bad."

the kite went up and up. soon it was nēar the clouds. jane yelled, "now I'm ōver the town, town, town, but I want to go down, down, down."

at last the kite came down, it landed in a farm five miles from town. jane left the kite there and walked back to her home. then she tōld her dad, "now I knōw whȳ, whȳ, whȳ I should not flȳ, flȳ, flȳ."

jane never tried flȳing again.

the end

159

the little cloud

there was a little cloud. the little cloud lived in the skȳ with a mother cloud and a father cloud.

the father cloud was very big and very dark. every now and then the father cloud would sāy, “it is time to make some rāin.” the father cloud would shake and make loud thunder sounds—“boom, boom.” then the rāin would fall from the cloud. the father cloud was very proud. he was the best rāin maker in the skȳ.

but the mother cloud was pretty good at māking rāin too. every now and then she would sāy, “I think I’ll make some rāin.” she would make some loud thunder sounds, and out would come the rāin.

but the little cloud could not make rāin. he would sāy, "I think I'll make some rāin." he would shake and shake. he would trȳ as hard as he could, but no rāin came from that small cloud.

the mother cloud said, "dōn't fēēl bad. when you are bigger, you will make rāin. you are too small now, but you will grōw."

and that small cloud did grōw. every dāy he got a little bigger and a little darker. and every dāy he trīed to make rāin. but he couldn't ēven make loud sounds. and not one drop of rāin came from that cloud. he felt very sad.

then one dāy something happened. the wind was blōwing very hard.

159

that wind bēgan to blōw the little cloud far awāy from his mother and father. he called to them. but they were māking loud sounds, so they couldn't hēar him.

more next time

the small cloud must help

the small cloud was far awāy from his father and mother. "I am so sad that I will crȳ," the cloud said. but when the cloud trīed to crȳ, no tēars came out. that made the cloud ēven sadder.

just then someone called, "help, help."

a small dēēr and a mother dēēr were nēar a big forest fire. the dēēr were trapped. "help, help," they called.

the little cloud called, "mom and dad, come ōver here and make some rāin on the forest." but they couldn't hēar him.

the little cloud said, "if I could make rāin, I could help those dēēr."

160

now the fire was all around the two dēēr. the cloud said, "I am the ōnly one who can help those dēēr. so I will trȳ to rāin."

the cloud began to shake. he became bigger and darker. "boom, boom," he said. then drops started to fall from the cloud. that rāin fell faster and faster. soon it sōaked the trēēs that were on fire, and it sōaked the two dēēr. all the fires were out.

"thank you, thank you," they called to the cloud.

just then the mother cloud and the father cloud flōated up to the little cloud. the father cloud said, "we see what you did. you are a good cloud."

the mother cloud said, "I am so proud. tōdāy mȳ little cloud became a rēal rāin cloud."

this is the end.